TO COURAGEOUSLY KNOW AND FOLLOW AFTER TRUTH

THE LIFE AND WORK OF MOTHER CATHERINE ABRIKOSOVA

SISTER MARY OF THE SACRED HEART, OP

2013
DNS PUBLICATIONS

To Courageously Know and Follow After Truth: The Life and Work of Mother Catherine Abrikosova
by Sister Mary of the Sacred Heart, OP

Copyright © 2013 Dominican Nuns of the
Perpetual Rosary
Summit, New Jersey

All rights reserved. No part of this book may be reproduced, stored in a retrieval system, or transmitted in any form, or by any means, electronic, mechanical, photocopying, recording or otherwise, without the prior written permission of the publisher, except by a reviewer, who may quote brief passages in a review.

Printed in the United States of America

DNS PUBLICATIONS
Dominican Nuns of Summit
543 Springfield Avenue
Summit, New Jersey 07901
www.nunsopsummit.org

ISBN: 0615785212
ISBN-13: 978-0615785219

Contents

Introduction 1
Early Life 7
Russian Byzantine Catholics 21
Moscow Mission 27
Communist Persecution 49
With Jesus on the Cross 105
Conclusion 111
Photographs 115
Prayer for Beatification 119
About the Author 121
Dominican Nuns of the Monastery of St. Jude
 123

Introduction

In his letter, "'Go tell my brothers!' Dominican women and evangelization," Fr. Bruno Cadoré states that "To speak of Dominican women—nuns, sisters, consecrated women and laity—is, before all else, to speak of the immense role that they have had and continue to have in this task of evangelization, in this engendering of hope through the evangelization of the 'word of God' in the world." One such Dominican woman who fully lived out the Dominican charism of evangelization is Mother Catherine Abrikosova, foundress of the Byzantine Dominican Sisters in Russia and martyr under Communism. In June 2002, the Catholic Bishops in Russia, during their *ad limina* visit to Rome, introduced the causes of several Catholic martyrs who suffered under Communism among whom are

Mother Catherine and Sister Rosa of the Heart of Mary, one of the Sisters.[1] Although well-known in the Order at the time of their founding, most Dominicans today have never heard of the Byzantine Dominicans in Russia. Fortunately several Russian books about them are in the process of being translated into English.[2]

In order to understand the influences that played a significant part in Mother Catherine's life, it would be useful to do a brief review of Russian Church history. Russia received Christianity through Byzantium, where the Emperor exercised almost complete control over all aspects of life, including the Church. This model was followed by the Russians, especially after the fall of Constantinople, when Moscow declared itself the "Third Rome" and the true inheritor of the Christian faith. The Tsar saw himself as "entrusted with the mission of defending

---

[1] Cf. http://en.catholicmartyrs.org/

[2] Professor Joseph Lake, TOP, has translated Mother's biography by Pavel Parfentiev, promoter of her cause, and it is presently at the publishers. Sister Maria Gemma, OP, of the Dominican Sisters of Mary, Mother of the Eucharist, has been working on the book *Coming to Love God and to Follow After Him*.

the *only true Church*....his role was on the same level as that of the hierarchy; it was founded on the firm belief that the ruling sovereign was indispensable to the Church."[3]

When Peter I became Tsar in 1698, the Church experienced a great crisis. Having spent considerable time in Western Europe where he became thoroughly imbued with the Enlightenment philosophies, Peter was determined to destroy the Old Russia and build a new one based on these ideas. He was quite ruthless and determined in his efforts and the Russian Orthodox Church was one of his earliest victims. His first step was to confiscate all Church and monastery properties and make them state properties. A significant number of them were closed. Likewise he enforced strict laws forbidding the teaching of the Orthodox faith outside of the Divine Services, restricting who could enter into monasteries[4] and the priesthood, and controlling the

---

[3] Helen Iswolsky, *Christ in Russia: The History, Tradition, and Life of the Russian Church* (Milwaukee: Bruce Publishing Co., 1960), 78-80.

[4] e.g. one had to be at least 50 years old before one could enter!

kind of formation and training priestly candidates could receive. When the Patriarch died in 1700 Peter abolished the Patriarchate and established a secular body to rule over the Russian Orthodox Church called the Holy Synod which was modeled on the Lutheran model. In reality it was the Tsar who was now head of the Russian Church.

Among the Enlightenment influences brought to Russia were secret societies which spread like wild fire, the most prominent being the Free Masons. Revolutionary ideas also began to take root, many of them with no real purpose except the goal of destroying all that was of the "old" way of life and establish a new one. These revolutionary ideas took root among the intelligentsia—the new ruling class Peter I had set up in Russia to replace the old Boyar system. Universities became the seed bed for revolutionary thought and actions. While there was some revival of the true Russian Orthodox faith in Russia from time to time, it played no significant part in the life of most of the Russian intelligentsia. It is true many of the young were seeking values by which they could live, but in those confusing times the Church itself was in a weak position and not able to exert much influence for the good.

Early Life

Mother Catherine was born Anna Ivanovna in Moscow on December 2, 1883 of the Abrikosov merchant family. The Merchant class in Russia had a unique importance at that time. As the bedrock of Russian society and of the Church, they were known not primarily for their wealth, but for the many philanthropic works they fostered—hospitals, schools, orphanages, etc. The Abrikosov[5] family, granted their family name in 1814, set up a candy company which also made fresh fruit preserves, mainly from apricots. It was Anna Ivanovna's grandfather, Aleksey Ivanovich, who built this into a prosperous business, which had factories in several

---

[5] The name comes from абрикос, which is Russian for apricot.

cities and even supplied candy to the Tsar.⁶ "There was nothing small in my grandfather. In all his deeds he showed the greatest nobility and was very moderate in his personal tastes, never indulging in the loose habits of most Moscow merchants, especially those whose sole aim was to make money."⁷

The oldest son, Nikolay Alexsevich, was more interested philosophy and science. It was Anna's father, Ivan Alexsevich, who took over the business. He also inherited his father's business acumen and is described as being "full of life, ever gay and loved by everyone."⁸ He and his wife already had 4 young sons and were hoping their next child would be a girl. Their prayer was answered but unfortunately Anna's mother died in giving birth to her, and her father died ten days later of tuberculosis of the throat contracted by handling "dirty money." Nikolay Alexsevich and his wife, who had six children of their own,

---

⁶ http://abrikosov-sons.ru/english. He was called the king of Russian candymaking.

⁷ Dimitrii I. Abrikossow, *Revelations of a Russian Diplomat, the Memoirs of Dmitrii I. Abrikossow* (Seattle: University of Washington Press, 1965), 6.

⁸ Ibid., 7.

immediately adopted the five little orphans, treating them as if they were their own children.

What little is known about Anna Ivanovna's childhood comes to us from her brother Dmitry Ivanovich's autobiography. He relates that his Uncle Nikolay and Aunt Vera were as loving as they were good. "Our childhood passed in an atmosphere of mutual confidence and love. We lived in a big house belonging to my grandfather, who was building a new house for himself."[9] In the summertime the family moved out to the country, as was the Russian custom, to a place called "the Oaks." As was also the custom, the children were educated at home by various tutors and governesses. Dmitry Ivanovich describes their childhood as carefree and joyous, and relates that their English governess was quite shocked at the close relationship between parents and children. In England, she used to tell them, children were seen and not heard![10]

---

[9] Ibid., 11. The grandfather and his wife Agrippina had 22 children, 17 of whom lived to adulthood and they all lived on the same street, taking up both sides!

[10] Cf. Ibid., 16.

Anna Ivanovna, who desired to be a teacher, studied at the First Women's Lyceum in Moscow and received the Gold Medal grade in 1899. While she was trying to continue her education at the university, the majority of the students treated her so badly that she became ill and had to leave. "Every day as I went into the room the girls would divide up the passage and stand aside not to brush me as I passed because they hated me as one of the privileged class."[11] Then she remembered her childhood dream of attending Girton College at Cambridge University and decided to go there in 1901. This was the first women's college in Great Britain, but unlike the universities in Russia, women were not allowed to actually receive any degrees. Her brother Dmitry Ivanovich accompanied her. He relates that they both were shocked when the headmistress informed them of the strict rules regulating the girls' behavior. In Russia they had been taught that England was the land of greatest liberty. If in Russia girls at the university had

---

[11] Pavel A. Parfentiev, *Mother Catherine, Life and Work* (St. Petersburg, RU: Keriga Publishing, 2004), Appendix I, "Letters of Dorothy Howard," 170.

been encumbered with such strictness, they would have protested mightily.[12]

One of her closest friends at Girton was Miss Dorothy Georgiana Howard and her letters home at this time give us our first real glimpses of Anna Ivanovna. First we learn how earnestly Anna loved her own country and how she longed to do something for the people. She was deeply moved by the plight of the poor and wanted to be a part of their fight for a better way of life. But at the same time she refused in conscience to join any of the radical groups, a decision which put her in conflict with her friends who did. In one of Miss Howard's letters we read about one such incident:

> The girl asked her, however, to attend a meeting, which Ania consented to. It was held in a sort of garret, of nasty appearance—one tiny window, low-roofed and so forth, and hardly any furniture. She says all the people looked ferocious, and she felt

---

[12] Cf. Abrikossow, 69.

as if she were going to be eaten. She had thought she was merely going to listen to their ordinary talk, when lo and behold, to her indignation she found that she was the center of the meeting, being held on trial for having stopped the peasants from further rioting! They asked her why she had done it and were apparently very angry. So she was angry too, and said it was monstrous of them to egg it on. They replied that it was just an opportune moment for rousing them up to rebel. The talk went on and finally they broke up the meeting saying that they would continue to take advantage as best they could of what had happened in the village, and try to stir the people up again.[13]

Anna Ivanovna exhibited the same courageous spirit at Girton when one of the girls kept a book that all the students needed for one of their papers.

---

[13] Parfentiev, "Letters," 173-174.

> We are 10 of us in our year and we have all been set the same essay to be done for Miss MacA. By Monday or Tuesday with only one book out of which we can read up the subject. This is a library book, Freeman's "Federal Government" and one of the girls, Miss Edwards has had this book for a week...One of the other girls went to ask for it but she said she hadn't finished it yet...and gave the same answer to several others. Finally she said "When I have done, I will give it to Miss Eccles" (another of our year)!! Then the ire of the Russian girl was roused and she said to her "Is it your very own book? This here is *my* book, I can give it to whomever I like—but that is of the library" and carried it off and put it back in the library.[14]

When Russia was undergoing a severe famine in 1902-1903 she was deeply afflicted and asked her friends at Girton for advice. She wanted in some way to return and set up a soup kitchen to help, but could

---

[14] Ibid., 169.

find no suitable way to do so. Her friends instead came up with another solution. They greatly admired the fine Russian embroidery Anna had which she said was very common among even the peasants, but which in England was very expensive. So Anna asked her family to send the embroidered goods, which her friends were able to sell to friends and family members and thus raise a considerable sum to send back home to Russia to help feed the poor.

Although the grandparents were very devout Orthodox believers, the grandchildren, influenced by the revolutionary ideas in the universities where they studied, had pretty much abandoned their faith. Anna was no exception. One summer she helped out in the school run by the local Russian Orthodox priest.

> Here she was getting on well, when the children found out that she was not strictly orthodox. So they asked her once, "Is there a hell." She said that there was not, or that it wasn't everlasting or something. Whereupon next Bible class from the priest when he was discoursing about

Hell the children piped up and said "Oh there is *no* such place." "Who says that?" thunders the priest. "Mistress does." Very well, Mistress is asked to interview his Reverence at once. "Mistress" is 17, and rather proud of her religious views, and so argues with his Reverence who soon ends up the visit and says no more. But presently "Mistress" hears from her uncle that his Reverence has written to him to say that he had better withdraw his niece or else he will have to inform the Government. Such was the humiliating end of the dreams of teaching rows of little children all that was interesting and beautiful and good![15]

At the end of two years, in 1903, she graduated from Girton with the equivalent of what would have been a bachelor's degree. Shortly after returning home to Moscow, Anna Ivanovna married her first cousin Vladimir Vladimirovich Abrikosov. Her brother Dmitry Ivanovich, who considered Anna as his best friend, was appalled and did everything he

---

[15] Ibid., 170.

could to dissuade her. It was unthinkable to him that a person as brilliant as Anna could marry someone whom in his opinion "had all my defects, without any of my virtues....I continued my attempts to change my sister's mind, not sparing in my letters the object of her affections, with the result that one day I received a short note in which she pointed out that I had forgotten one thing, namely that she loved him. It was the end of our friendship."[16]

Vladimir Vladimirovich, like herself, had majored in history and philosophy in the University. Their main interest being Western European civilization, they left Russia and spent the next 5 years traveling throughout France, Italy and Switzerland. Visits to museums and monasteries as part of their interest in history brought them into contact with Roman Catholicism. As Vladimir Vladimovich later wrote: "[I]n the Catholic form of Christianity we found the solution to questions about the meaning of life which up to then we had not been able to find in other theories; we were not acquainted with

---

[16] Abrikossow, 131.

Orthodoxy, and didn't even attend church. We did not deny the existence of God, but we did not believe either; we lived without God. The impulse for my wife…and for me too…was the strong influence coming from Western culture."[17]

In Rome they visited Princess Maria Mikhailovna Volkonsky, a well-known convert to Catholicism. It was here that Anna Ivanovna read the *Dialogue* of St. Catherine of Siena and fell deeply in love with the Dominican Charism of truth. "The profound nature of the teaching of the Dominican saint as reflected in her famous work gripped the young traveler. She was especially moved, as she was later to say, by her words 'to courageously know and to follow after truth.'"[18]

She eagerly pursued her new goal to learn more about Catholicism and in particular the Dominican Order. In 1908, while in Paris, she requested reception into the Catholic Church from

---

[17] Parfentiev, Letter of Fr. Vladimir, 24.
[18] Parfentiev, 26.

Fr. Maurice Riviére. On December 20th of that year she was solemnly received into the Church in the Chapel of the Daughters of Charity of St. Vincent de Paul. Although she wanted to remain in the Latin rite, Fr. Riviére reminded her that from the canonical point of view she belonged to the Byzantine Slavonic Rite.[19] Vladimir for his part, though he did not oppose his wife's actions, showed some anti-Catholicism during this process. He also began to attend the Divine Liturgy in the Russian Orthodox Church, something he had never done before. While they continued their travels Anna Ivanovna read Fr. Henri Lacordaire's *Life of St. Dominic*, thus deepening her love for Dominican life. To her great joy Vladimir eventually began to show more interest in the Catholic Church and on November 23rd, 1909, in the same chapel of St. Vincent de Paul, he was received into the Catholic Church.

The Abrikosovs submitted a petition to Pope Pius X to be allowed to remain in the Latin rite.

---

[19] *Orientalium Dignitas* of Pope Pius X. Cf. http://www.papalencyclicals.net/Leo13/l13orient.htm

However, the Pope, after reminding them that according to Canon Law[20] Russians must remain within their own Byzantine rite when entering into the Catholic Church, "let it be known that the couple had the right temporarily to follow the Latin Rite, but that they must belong to the Eastern."[21] Although this answer was a great disappointment for them at the time, later they expressed great thanksgiving for this "glorious reply of Pius X." One of their major reasons, as Anna expressed it, was the poor quality of the Russian Orthodox clergy, which as we saw earlier was due to the fact that they were not permitted to study theology, etc., as was needed for proper training. Soon after this they were summoned back to Moscow by relatives around Christmas 1910, and except for one brief trip, remained in Russia thereafter.

---

[20] Ibid.
[21] Parfentiev, 30.

Russian Byzantine Catholics

It will be helpful at this point to take a quick look at the Russian Byzantine Catholic Church. First of all, it is to be noted that the disputes between Rome and Constantinople did not directly involve the Russian Orthodox Church. At that time they were suffering from invasions of the Tartars and their main focus was survival. In 1439 Metropolitan Isidore of Kyiv, with full approval of the Tsar, attended the Council of Florence along with several members of his hierarchy, the Patriarch of Constantinople and other Eastern Church representatives of other countries. All delegates having signed the Act of Union, the Russians returned home and in the presence of Tsar Basil II celebrated the Divine Liturgy on March 19, 1441 in thanksgiving for such a grace. There was much rejoicing among the people, but inexplicitly four days later, the Tsar suddenly became enraged, declared the Act of Union invalid, and sent troops to arrest the Metropolitan. He was able to escape having been forewarned, and continued to maintain union with Rome with a small group of faithful.[22] These people secretly remained in union with Rome even though the Tsar issued a decree that all Catholics, including foreign ones, would be subject to exile or even death. In the eighteenth century several Russians, such as Princess Elizabeth Gallitzin (1748-1806) and her son, Dmitri Augustine, entered the Church, an action which entailed exile.[23]

Two of the most famous converts in the nineteenth century were Princess Zinaida G. Volkonsky[24] and the philosopher Vladimir Soloviev. Princess Zinaida, even though active in the court life

---

[22] Rev. Christopher Zugger, *The Forgotten Catholics of the Soviet Empire from Lenin through Stalin* (Syracuse: Syracuse University Press, 2001), 82.

[23] 1770-1840. Dmitri came to the United States, was ordained a priest, and worked for many decades as the Apostle of the Alleghanies. His cause for canonization has been introduced in Rome.

[24] The Volkonskys were one of the oldest and most influential princely families in Russia. Zinaida's brother-in-law was one of the leaders of the Decembrist movement. Two of her sons, Peter and Alexandr eventually became Catholics, with Peter later becoming a priest and working with Cardinal Sheptitsky.

of the Tsar and his family, had a great love for truth and interest in history. She began her own investigation of Church history and was amazed to find that the translation the Russian Orthodox had of the Church fathers was often different from that of the original language. In fact, especially regarding the role of the Pope, the Russian translation was often in distinct contradiction. She then set herself to compile a two volume historical/theological work showing that the Roman Catholic Church was indeed that which was founded by Christ. She is thus considered the first woman theologian of Russia. Her new-found interest in the Catholic Church causing suspicion in the court, she and one of her sons went to Rome where she took up residence. Eventually she became a Franciscan Tertiary and spent her life caring for the poor in Rome.

Vladimir Soloviev from St. Petersburg, was a famous professor of philosophy and was regarded as the '"philosopher of the Godmanhood,' i.e., the union of God with man and man with God."[25] After years of struggling to find the truth, he discovered it in the Catholic Church. He openly wrote and talked about the Catholic Church as being the true Church founded by Christ. For this he was forbidden to teach in any of the Universities in Russia. According to Soloviev's reasoning, the Russian Orthodox Church is separated from the Holy See only *de facto* (there was no direct formal breach between the Sees of Rome and Moscow), so that one can profess the totality of Catholic doctrine and be in communion with the Holy See while continuing to be Russian Orthodox. Soloviev was secretly received into communion with the Holy See as a Russian Byzantine Catholic on February 18, 1896 by Fr. Nicholas Tolstoy, the first Russian Byzantine Catholic priest (see below). Soloviev's thought had a profound impact on several generations of Russian society and inspired such later thinkers as Fr. S. Bulgakov and Fr. P. Florensky. Soloviev has been called by some the Russian

---

[25] http://cssronline.org/CSSR/Current/Articles%20-%20Likoudis.pdf

Newman.[26] Pope John Paul II read Soloviev as a young man and was profoundly influenced by him. He strongly recommended his writings especially in his encyclical, *Fides et Ratio*.

In 1893, Fr. Nicholas Tolstoy, a Russian Orthodox priest and chaplain of the Imperial Court, was received into communion with the See of Rome and was incardinated in the Melkite Catholic church. He returned to St. Petersburg and a small community began to form around him. Larger numbers of like-minded individuals began to form circles and communities in St. Petersburg and Moscow and among them were a number of Russian Orthodox clergy, as well as some Russian Old Ritualist or Old Believer priests. Several young men became Russian Byzantine priests—Fr. Ivan Deubner, Fr. Alexander Zerchaninov and Fr. Eustachios Susalev. One of the most prominent and active members was Miss Natalia Sergeyevna Ushakova, a niece of the Prime Minister

---

[26] He was a close friend of Princess Maria Volkonsky. Although Anna Ivanovna and Princess Maria remained life-long friends and in constant communication, it is unknown how much of an influence Soloviev was in her life and thinking. Most of her writings were confiscated by the KGB.

Stolypin. She was able to use her influence with the government to obtain certain privileges for Byzantine Catholics such as permission to use an apartment for a chapel for the Divine Services. Prince Peter and Princess Maria also used their influence as much as they could. Finally, the decree of Religious Tolerance of the Tsar in 1905 allowed Russians to become Catholics although with great difficulties involved. This enabled the Vatican to appoint Fr. Alexander as Administrator of the Mission to Russian Byzantine Catholics on May 22, 1908.

On April 29, 1909, Easter Sunday in the Orthodox calendar, the three Russian Byzantine priests publicly celebrated the Easter Liturgy and then sent a telegram to the Tsar with Easter greetings. This was received favorably and for a time harassment from the secret police ceased. In April 1911 Miss Ushakova obtained from the Prime Minister legal authorization to move the Chapel to a larger apartment. This was the situation when the Abrikosovs came back to Russia.

Moscow Mission

Upon returning home to Moscow in 1910, Anna Ivanovna and Vladimir Vladimirovich began what they called their "Moscow Mission." Their family and acquaintances having ostracized them for becoming Catholics, they bought a large apartment for themselves and began conducting missionary work. Various groups—social, philosophical, political—would hold meetings, give talks or lectures followed by discussions over tea. These were very popular in Russia, and soon the Abrikosovs had quite a large group attending these meetings. Anna Ivanovna would hold discussions on asceticism, mysticism and Church history while Vladimir Vladimorich would take care of philosophical and dogmatic topics. They both knew quite a few languages and Anna would read Catholic books in French, Italian, German, English and Latin in order to learn more of the Catholic faith. She also began translating some of these works into Russian. "They had found the Truth for themselves and now they wanted to help their fellow countrymen do the same."[27] The youthful desire of Anna Ivanovana to teach others what was "beautiful and good" was finally coming true.

Sister Josafata[28] gives us a wonderful description of Anna Ivanovna from about this time period.

> Against this background the figure of Anna Ivanovna stands out in a sharply defined way: a woman of high Catholic culture of mind and heart, supernatural principles applied to herself, to people, and to the world. It felt as if the wealthy surroundings were simply an exterior setting in which she was temporarily encased and with the help of which she served God. In so far as I remember I

---

[27] Parfentiev, 42.
[28] Entered the Sisters but remained a Dominican Tertiary member.

unfailingly sensed in her a freedom and an elevation of spirit; she knew how to remain faithful to God whether in wealth or poverty, sickness or humiliation. This was a free soul, soaring like an eagle, one which from its first steps of its newly conscious life labored greatly for God, and received much from Him in return.

  Now we should say something about Anna Ivanovna's physical appearance. She was of medium height; her figure was well-proportioned, built solidly; hair light brown; face large and rather thin, very expressive, with a radiant, high forehead, prominent cheekbones, and an aquiline nose. The eyes were expressive, peaceful and penetrating; the corners of her mouth bespoke strength of character, and her smile, kindness and joy of spirit. Anna Ivanovna's face in profile recalled that of Savonarola in the portraits. Her walk was measured, her movements calm, her head always raised somewhat. She dressed simply, severely, always in black and white, always tastefully. In a word, she had the appearance of a noble matron.

Anna Ivanovna spoke French, Italian, English, and German fluently; she understood Latin and Greek. From the moment of her conversion she read literature in these languages constantly and lots of it. She studied different areas, first those of general Catholic content, later especially things connected with the Dominicans. Her mind was exalted and serene. Her spiritual life and her Dominican practice inspired her and made her thinking process more precise. She was kind, responsive, sensitive, and warm, but without sentimentality and familiarity. She tended to be good-heartedly humorous. She had a wonderful ability to combine good common sense with supernatural principles, and this is what made her a good spiritual director. She did not talk a lot—she expressed herself concisely, simply, and wittily. She was observant and a good psychologist.[29]

---

[29] As quoted in Parfentiev, 40-41.

One of Anna's first new friends was Natalya Sergeyevna Roznanov, who was the first Dominican Tertiary in Moscow. She introduced the Abrikosovs to the pastor of the Church of St. Louis, Fr. Albert Libercier, OP. In 1911 he received Anna into the Dominican Third Order Novitiate and for her religious name she took Sr. Mary Catherine of Siena. In 1914 Vladimir also entered the Dominican novitiate taking the name Brother Thomas Aquinas. Since there was no Byzantine rite priest in Moscow at this time, they belonged to the parish of Sts. Peter and Paul.

In 1910 and again in 1911 Blessed Leonid Federov[30] visited the Abrikosovs in Moscow. Blessed Leonid, at this time still in the seminary, came incognito to Russia for Metropolitan (later Cardinal) Andrew Sheptitsky,[31] head of the Ukrainian Greek Catholic Church, to keep up contact with the

---

[30] Beatified by Pope John Paul II in Ukraine, June 2001.

[31] The Servant of God, Andrew Sheptitsky was by decree of Pope Pius X the head of all Byzantine Catholics in the Russian Empire.

Byzantine rite Catholics and see how things were going. Leonid, even as a young boy, was intensely fervent in his Russian Orthodox faith and began studies to become a priest. But through frequent discussions with the Catholics who frequented his widowed mother's restaurant, he came to accept that the Catholic Church was truly the Church instituted by Christ. With the assistance of Metropolitan Sheptitsky and blessing of his spiritual father, he left Russia to continue his studies. But because the Tsar's secret police were keeping watch on him, he had to change his name and location several times. After being in Rome for a time he was sent secretly to the Dominican "Albertinum" in Fribourg to continue his studies. His mother constantly supported him and herself became a Catholic in 1908, remaining in the Byzantine rite. Metropolitan Sheptitsky arranged for Leonid's ordination as a Byzantine rite priest to take place in Constantinople by a Bulgarian Catholic Bishop in 1911.

The first meetings were quite favorable on both sides. It was during the second meeting in 1911 that Vladimir secretly told Father Leonid of his desire to be ordained a priest and asked which books he needed to study for this purpose. The Abrikosovs were gradually falling more and more in love with their own Byzantine heritage. Blessed Leonid wrote in a letter to Metropolitan Sheptitsky in February 11, 1911:

> On the subject of this family one can say with the Apostle Paul, "I greet their domestic church." In few places can one meet young people in the flower of their strength so dedicated to the cause of the Church and so religious. They disseminate Catholicism among their circle of acquaintances with all the resources at their disposal: influence, material aid, and the like. Abrikosov's wife, Anna Ivanovna, busies herself from morning to night with the children of the Russian Catholics, goes to visit people she knows, receives them in her home with the sole aim of converting them to Catholicism. Her husband Vladimir Vladimirovich does the same. He secretly told me about

his desire to become a priest, and asked that I show him the textbooks which would be needed. He speaks French well, and knows German, Italian, Latin, and a little Greek. The upright character of both of them and their strict way of life in total conformity with all the precepts of the Church make them rare people in our times.[32]

The Abrikosovs spent the summer of 1913 abroad, including some time in Rome where they took their vows as Dominican tertiaries in the hands of the Procurator General, Fr. Desqueyrous, O.P. During this same time Anna and Vladimir took the vow of chastity so as to be better able to carry out what seemed clearly God's will. They were granted a private audience with Pope Pius X who wholeheartedly approved of their Russian apostolate. But upon their return to Moscow tensions began to build between themselves and the Byzantine Catholics in St. Petersburg. The main bone of contention was a journal the Catholics in St. Petersburg began to

---

[32] Letter of Blessed Leonid as quoted by Parfentiev, 44.

publish called "Word of Truth." In it they expounded the ideas of Vladimir Soloviev on the truly Catholic view of Church unity by showing complete adherence to Orthodox traditions. They also had received instructions and permissions from Cardinal Merry del Val, Secretary of State to Pope Pius X, to adhere to synodal[33] customs in the Liturgy.

Fr. Ignaty Chayesvsky, the Polish pastor at Sts. Peter and Paul in Moscow, and who seemed to be favorable to Byzantine rite Russians, was particularly displeased and disapproved wholeheartedly of their publication and practices. Anna Ivanovna wrote a letter of protest to the editor along the same lines. It is a sad fact that the greater majority of the Latin rite clergy did not understand nor approve of the Eastern Churches at all. Unfortunately this was especially true of the Polish clergy, and even Dominicans working in Russia belonged to the view that the only true rite was the Latin rite. The view was held that the Byzantine rite was to be tolerated as "a necessary evil," and a

---

[33] That is, the liturgical customs as promulgated by the Holy Synod, the secular ruling body of the Russian Orthodox Church.

means of bringing them eventually into the Latin rite. They firmly believed that in time the Orthodox/Byzantine rite would disappear. Unfortunately this view still exists even in our own times.[34]

Fr. Leonid arrived in St. Petersburg toward the end of 1913, and together with Natalya Sergeyevna Ushakov and a man identified only as Kharichev, traveled to Moscow and met with the Abrikosovs. Unfortunately the meeting did not go well and Anna and Vladimir were quite unfriendly to Miss Ushakov. Natalya Sergeyevna and Kharichev left at the end of the first day, with Natalya saying to Fr. Leonid, "They are either not mature—or overripe. They need to be left alone, so they don't bite."[35] Fr. Leonid stayed on a few days and tried to explain the true situation, but it seemed to be all in vain. In a subsequent letter to Metropolitan Sheptitsky, Fr. Leonid wrote:

---

[34] I was told by a Polish Dominican working in Russia that the establishment of the Byzantine Dominican Sisters was a terrible mistake and one best forgotten.

[35] Letter of Blessed Leonid as quoted by Parfentiev, 55.

> The St. Petersburg Catholics were of course as one in wanting to be in lively contact with their brothers and sisters in Moscow, and they asked me to facilitate this. Naturally this is what I too wanted. We went to Moscow as a threesome: Kharichev, Ushakov, and I. The Abrikosovs received us warmly and cordially. Kharichev was introduced to them and made a good impression. They spoke relatively little with Natalya Sergeyevna, and they disagreed with her, although in my opinion they were not totally open. The real arguments started only after the departure of Kharichev and Ushakov, when we were left face to face and spoke with one another for an entire week.[36]

Further in the letter Fr. Leonid explains their main objection was that there was no official Church approval.

---

[36] Ibid., 55.

We do not submit to Church authority, because our journal ("Word of Truth") appears without its approval….Gradually our discussion got down to the basic questions of principle. And it is here that you can see all the difficulty of my position. For all my insistence that the term "Catholic/Universal" had been approved, and that the journal itself had been approved….I tried earnestly to explain to them that in our position there could be no question of any official piece of paper, since we find ourselves in the most hopeless of situations: the discovery of such a paper by the government would be tantamount to the suicide of the Mission. They cannot understand this, and think that the lives of contemporary Russian Catholics ought to and must proceed in the same circumstances as the lives in any well-established Catholic parish. Chayevsky, of course, supports them in this….Closed within their small circle, isolated from the people and not having the least notion of their mood and needs, they are like the most elegant, fine little china statues with which the ladies of the court of Louis XV adorned their little shelves. "Holiness! Holiness!" they repeat like parrots. Their fanaticism reaches an extreme. One cannot read books from the Synod, one cannot read Catholic books translated into Russian if the Synod has given them its approval. To enter a schismatic church means to sully one's self and have to do with a "crowd of heretics". That this is allowed they do not wish to believe. They do not even believe in the instruction to adhere strictly to Synodal custom, as this is expressed in the letter of Cardinal Merry del Val to Metropolitan Denisevich. They view the favorable relationship of the bishops and priests to "The Word of Truth" askance and find it entirely proper to the "Age of Modernism"—since after all certain journals come out for years on end, and are only then forbidden.[37]

The outbreak of World War I brought an easement of the tensions as everyone's attention was

---

[37] Ibid., 56.

on the events surrounding the war. On his fourth visit to Russia in 1914, Fr. Leonid, being considered "harmful to state security" for his connections with Metropolitan Sheptitsky, was arrested by the Tsar's police, exiled to Siberia and kept under surveillance. In September of that year Russian forces attacked and occupied Western Ukraine.[38] One of the goals of the Russian government was to destroy the Ukrainian Greek Catholic Church and many churches were shut down while priests were arrested and exiled. On the 15th of September Metropolitan Andrey Sheptitsky, as head of the Ukrainian Greek Catholics, was arrested and imprisoned.

During these years, the majority of persons coming to the lectures were young women. Several of these also wished to become Dominican Tertiaries and so Anna Ivanovna and Fr. Libercier began the process of formation. Except for a few Polish women, most of them were from Russian Orthodox families and had entered the Catholic Church. It was

---

[38] The western part of Ukraine was at that time under Austrian control, and at the beginning of the war Russia invaded in order to attack Austria.

quite an arduous ordeal for them. First of all one had to give the government authorities an official declaration of their desire to convert to Catholicism. The authorities would then send an Orthodox priest who would admonish and threaten them for taking such a dangerous step. Many families would force the girls out of the home, and so Anna and Vladimir would take them in. For example, Raisa Krylyovsky (later Sr. Margaret of Hungary) was first imprisoned in her room at home and not allowed to take food or drink. When she persisted in her desire, they turned her out with only the clothes she was wearing. Anna Ivanovna, as being the cause for their desire to convert also was made to suffer much from both the authorities and families.

Even with all that was going on, Anna Ivanovna continued translating many books into Russian among them the *Life of St. Catherine*, Litany of St. Dominic, and the *Life of St. Dominic* by Lacordaire, the last two of which still exist and have been republished several times. She also translated from the French Fr. Rousset's "Guide for the Brothers and

Sisters of the Third Order of Penance of St. Dominic."

The revolution and establishment of the Provisional Government in March 1917 brought great hope among both Catholics and the Russian Orthodox. One of the first decrees was "The Abolition of Religious and Nationality Restrictions." This allowed for complete freedom for all and both Churches made good use of this "breath of freedom." The Orthodox held a council, elected a Patriarch and reestablished the Church free from government control. The new Patriarch also exhibited a favorable attitude toward the Byzantine Catholics.

Both Metropolitan Sheptitsky and Fr. Leonid were released from prison that March and they went straight to St. Petersburg. Metropolitan Sheptitsky, with full powers granted to him by Pope Pius X, called a Council of the Russian Byzantine Church to establish an exarchate. The Abrikosovs came from Moscow to attend, and Sheptitsky ordained Vladimir to the priesthood in the Maltese Chapel on June 11,

1917. The Council was then immediately convened in the ceremonial hall of the church of St. Catherine of Alexandria[39] with all the Eastern Rite clergy present. He appointed Fr. Leonid as the First Exarch of the Byzantine Catholics in Russia. At the final Session on June 13th, the entire hierarchy of the Latin Rite was also present. The public proclamation of the establishment of the Exarchate was read at this meeting and the Council Acts were sent to Rome. Official confirmation by Pope Benedict XV was given on March 21, 1921 by the papal decree "Ex Amplissimo" which recognized the authority of the new Exarch and granted him the title of "prothonotary of the Apostolic See."[40]

Anna Ivanovna was present at the ordination of Fr. Vladimir, but it is not known whether she was present also at the Council meetings. However she did meet with Cardinal Sheptitsky and completely changed her opinion of him—"This is a holy man,

---

[39] This Church then and now belonged to the Dominican Order.

[40] Parfentiev, 68.

and a churchman in the full sense of the word. We have been entirely wrong on his account."[41] She was also more favorable to Fr. Leonid saying in a letter that he was a "uniquely gifted man, endowed with rare gifts as a missionary, remarkable talent at apologetics, a profound knowledge of the Russian people, with its spiritual needs, demands, and hopes."[42] Later Anna remarked about Miss Ushakov—"We made fun of her but how right she was at the time!"[43] These words show how truly Anna sought to live her motto—"to have the courage to know and follow after the truth." What a difference there was in the Abrikosovs since 1914. Now instead of being Latin Catholics trying to embrace some of their Russian heritage, they were truly and completely Russian Catholics!

After the Council Fr. Vladimir and Anna returned to Moscow filled with renewed vigor. The care of all Byzantine Catholics in Moscow was now

---

[41] Ibid., 67.
[42] Ibid.
[43] Ibid.

committed to Fr. Vladimir's care and he spent himself tirelessly in this cause. They set up a large room in their apartment as a Chapel for the celebration of the Divine Liturgy dedicated to the Nativity of the Blessed Virgin Mary. They saw even more clearly that Byzantine Catholics were the primary means for the reunion of Russia with the Universal Church.

The young women, both those living with the Abrikosovs and those who visited regularly, expressed the desire to live religious life. Hence on the 17th of August, 1917, Feast of St. Hyacinth, the young women met together to establish a religious community and chose Anna Ivanovna to be their superior. From this point on Anna became Mother Mary Catherine of Siena. "The Sisters (as they were now called) 'wished to realize the dream of their founder to go to the East to preach the Gospel and attain martyrdom.'" At first they followed Fr. Rousset's *Guide* but Mother Catherine also contacted communities of Dominican Sisters outside of Russia for help in setting up a new community. It was a new venture and challenge—to adapt Dominican life in a

Byzantine form and for this purpose they constantly sought guidance from the Dominican Curia in Rome. Sr. Iosafata relates: "Anna Ivanovna made an exhaustive study of the Eastern Rite and followed it scrupulously. The Third Order Dominican Sisters did the same. But at the same time in their personal devotions they made free use of certain Latin practices[44] such as bowing before the Blessed Sacrament, saying the rosary, doing the Stations of the Cross. They did their meditative prayer following both the eastern and the western ways."[45]

Fr. Verbitsky, although a Latin rite Pole, was an expert in Russian chant and helped Fr. Vladimir who was not musically talented. One of the parishioners Dmitri Kuz'min-Karaveyev, left this interesting account of Sister Imelda[46] and Fr. Vladimir:

---

[44] This should not be seen as an effort of Latinization, but rather since the Sisters were following the Constitutions of a Latin Rite community, they used the practices enjoined therein. It is thought that if they had been allowed to develop under normal conditions, they would have most certainly written their own Constitutions in due time.

[45] Parfentiev, 74.

[46] Her name before entering religious life was Anna Spiridonovna.

Her face was purely Russian, but with strikingly definite features. She was Director of the Sisters' choir, and when she began the troparion with her ringing voice it was impossible not to take her for the head of an Old Believer community. It should be remembered that it was customary in our community to sing in unison. To continue in this tone, really Anna Spiridonovna should be called not just a leader, but also the interpreter of the Community Rule. Every evening she would come to see Fr. Vladimir to determine the liturgy of the following day. It must be admitted that she knew the rubrics and liturgical books better than our Pastor, and I would often be struck when I had occasion to stay late at Fr. Vladimir's to see the respectful determination with which she would bring him up to the point which had already been decided upon by her in advance.[47]

---

[47] Parfentiev, 77-78.

Exarch Leonid had a high regard for Fr. Vladimir and in one of his letters wrote to Metropolitan Sheptitsky that he "is becoming a genuine Eastern priest with a hint of the Old Believer about him. There are steady conversions; discipline in the parish is model."[48]

---

[48] Ibid.

Communist Persecution

When the Communists took over in November 1917, the country was plunged into Civil War with the usual results of famine and disease afflicting the whole population. There was little food available to anyone. The Sisters had to work in order to make enough money for their basic needs. Almost all the Sisters had graduated from the university or had some higher education. For example, Sr. Catherine Ricci the Younger became a professor of Roman Philology at the University. But the Sisters never neglected their religious duties and continued as best they could with regular observance and growing in their understanding of religious life. Mother Catherine could see the Sisters needed special training to take them through the difficult times ahead.

Fr. Vladimir together with his father was arrested on October 23, 1918 and put in Butyrka prison, with no reason being given. When Mother Catherine visited him on November 17th, she told him that on November 2nd the Cheka had issued a decree for his release, but it had not been implemented. Fr. Vladimir then wrote to the Political Red Cross after which he was freed.

Around the beginning of the Revolution some of the Sisters took a vow offering their lives for Russia. Later all of them voluntarily made this same vow, which goes as follows:

> *To the honor and glory of Almighty God, Father, Son, and Holy Spirit, and of the ever blessed Virgin Mary and St. Dominic, we, consecrated Sisters Tertiaries of the Order of Preachers of Moscow Province of St. Dominic, surrender our lives to the last drop of blood, in sacrifice to the Holy Trinity for the salvation of Russia and for priests. In which may we be aided by Our Lord Jesus Christ, His Blessed Mother, our Holy*

Father Dominic, and all the saints of the Order of Friars Preachers. Amen.[49]

On October 25, 1919 the Civil War reached Moscow. For ten days the Sisters prayed in their chapel while war, death and destruction raged in the streets. Often they could hear the footsteps of soldiers coming for neighbors who were taken out in the street and shot.

Despite all this, the Sisters and parishioners went on with life. After the fighting had stopped, the Sisters continued their festive meal after the Divine Liturgy on Sundays and Feast days. Although food was hard to come by, they managed to find substitutions for tea and other items. Many people came regularly to the weekly sessions including Russian Orthodox clergy and such persons as the famous philosopher Nikolay Berdyaev. He brought his wife, who felt a strong attraction to the Catholic Faith and in time she became a Catholic. The Sisters did what they could for children, elderly and the sick,

---

[49] Parfentiev, 74.

though they themselves did not have even the essentials at times. The Vatican also set up an aid program called "Pro Russia" which sent them food and medicines, etc.

Because of all the work and the strain (one never knew when GPU would visit and search the apartments) Fr. Vladimir became greatly ill several times, and it seemed to Mother Catherine that he would die. Yet he was still able to prepare one of the young men of the parish for the priesthood, Nikolay Aleksandrov, who was ordained by Bishop Cieplak in St. Petersburg on August 1921. Nikolay was also a Dominican tertiary taking the name of Peter Martyr.

The Sisters grew in number and fervor, and the landlords gave them three more rooms, which still were not enough to hold everyone. In 1922 Exarch Feoderov asked Mother Catherine if some of the Sisters could come to St. Petersburg to start another Dominican monastic community there. Mother Catherine felt she had to refuse and he agreed with her reasons—there were not enough experienced

Sisters for the task. According to the Sisters' memoirs by 1922 there were about 25 fully professed young women living at the apartment. Besides these, there were also postulants preparing for eventual entry into the Community.

Sr. Josafata leaves this wonderful testimony about the life of the Sisters at this time:

> The liturgical life of the Sisters and their reverence for the Sacred Mysteries were especially amazing. I know several people who were so moved by these Dominican Masses that they made the decision to begin to lead a profound spiritual life from that time on. There was perpetual adoration of the Blessed Sacrament, uninterrupted day and night, in the chapel of the Order, also the parish church, during these last years. The Sisters took turns at adoration. They changed with each other every hour. During the day parishioners also signed up for adoration, but they did it in their own order.

The Sisters never wore the habit of the order,[50] but rather the same black dress with a white collar. Within the Community the Sisters wore crosses, medium sized, which had been sent to them from abroad. The Sisters wore white on feast days and on the feasts of the Order. The Dominican feast days were celebrated with solemnity and simplicity. The Sisters would be dressed and be happy in a way befitting the holiday. The atmosphere in the chapel would be happy—one could sense immediately that the day was some Dominican feast day. I need to emphasize one more trait which attracted the attention of those who observed the Community. This was their joyful and free obedience to superiors. To put it in a word, the Sisters were angels. They were so responsive to their monastic superiors that there was nothing forced or self-abasing about it. Rather it was a free, genuine and true act of obedience. I learned through personal experience that the

---

[50] Even in Tsarist Russia it was forbidden for religious to wear the Habit.

nun like these third order Dominicans is a very important model for apostolic work among the Russian intelligentsia. The frame of mind, the joy even of the Sister, her simplicity, decisiveness and at the same time her exalted convictions, her self-denial and spirit of sacrifice, all this produces a very positive and deep impression.[51]

Sister Josafata relates how faithful the Sisters were to observance of study, the older ones instructing the younger as needed especially in their own specialized field. Many of the Sisters were highly skilled, one of them even teaching at the seminary. For example, we read:

> One of the Sisters, Sr. Dominic (Valentina Sapozhnikov), was a specialist in Romance Philology. She was especially interested in Dante and medieval literature. She knew Dante so well that from 1917 to 1922 she was head of the program in the poetry of Dante at the University. She had written her thesis on Dante. She

---
[51] Parfentiev, 105.

shared the beauty and the profound religious feeling of Dante with the Sisters and the parishioners. She gave many lectures at the parish. Besides this she taught classes on scholastic philosophy and dogmatic theology, for example "On the Holy Trinity."[52]

About Mother Catherine Sr. Josafata wrote:

In Mother Catherine's apostolic work and in her approach to things spiritual the following gifts of grace were especially apparent: her unshakable faith, her sound reasoning, courage, a gift of wisdom and the ability to counsel. These works of hers also produced a strong impression because in addition to the qualities we have mentioned they are distinguished by a profound knowledge of the human soul, and they respect the psychological needs of today's believer. Among other works she wrote the following: "The Seven Last Words of Our Savior on the Cross", "The Mass of St. Dominic", "The Mother of God's Care" and "Go

---

[52] Ibid., 101-104.

Forth and Teach" (On the Feast of Sts. Peter and Paul).

No obstacles, difficulties, or sacrifices bothered her. She forged ahead with courage and without fear, and not fearing to take upon herself responsibility for them she led her spiritual daughters behind her. Even though these girls were menaced by prison and exile because they belonged to the Community, Mother did not hesitate to accept new Sisters, if she saw in them a true vocation. Of course she did warn them about the possibility of persecution and suffering. She was sensitive, warm, and magnanimous with those for whom she served as spiritual guide. She was also direct and determined, and she was demanding when it was necessary.

One young secular Moscow poet wrote of her that "she exuded the cool air of the mountain summits." It is a fine poetic comparison. Secular people, far removed from the life of the spirit, could certainly perceive Anna Ivanovna's personality that way. Mother was a person with a definite goal, and this was reflected in her spiritual life. She was consequent in everything, and her principles and inclinations were governed by the supernatural. So it was that she looked at life as if she saw it from the mountain summit, and surrounding her this cool made itself felt. Secular people often think of love for one's neighbor as acceptance unguided by any principle and as sentimental familiarity. The spiritual children of M. Catherine knew more closely the burning love, tenderness, and greatness of her heart. I myself had the great fortune to be her spiritual daughter for two years.[53]

Sr. Josafata mentions Mother Catherine's ability to see and understand the needs of each soul entrusted to her care. In Mother's meditations on the Seven Last Words, we see illustrated how profoundly she understood that each person was a unique individual and needed to be treated as such.

---

[53] Ibid., 106.

After the final renunciation of the created world comes a certain decisive time in one's life. Sometimes the Lord does not bring the soul to it immediately. He gives it a time for preparation and fills it with joy at His presence, but only in order afterward to lead it into the great solitude. We must keep it always in view that God wants our union with Him, and disposes everything else toward that goal. He is so careful of the individuality of each soul, He so respects and values it, that He gives each soul what is necessary for it to achieve union with Him in the most direct and quickest way. Each progression of the soul is like a new artistic creation of God, His free act of creativity. There are periods in the life of each soul which almost have to be repeated, but they too play themselves out differently. For some souls they are constant over the course of several years, for others they alternate with experiences of another order. But we have to know and believe that God disposes everything for the benefit of each individual soul. Thus, for example, the period of spiritual growth which I call the great solitude—which could not be more apposite to the Fourth Word of our Lord—is repeated in the life of almost every soul precisely because it is absolutely essential for our moving ahead. It is like a touchstone of good will, sincerity, and righteousness of soul, showing how willing it actually is to renounce everything and to bear all things for the sake of glorifying God by uniting itself with Him.[54]

In 1921 the Order sent a letter establishing Fr. Vladimir as official superior of the Tertiaries and gave him permission to accept candidates into the novitiate. In November 1922 Fr. Jean-Baptiste Amoundru, O.P., the only Dominican left in St. Petersburg by this time, visited the community. He was very pleased with all they were doing and "at their request wrote to the Master General and asked that they be formally recognized."[55] This formal recognition came in March 1923, approving them as a Dominican religious community. Fr. Amoudru was

---

[54] Ibid., Appendix III, "Seven Last Words," 194.
[55] Ibid., 82.

appointed as Vicar for the Master over the community and he visited them again in June 1923. In August he decided to begin visiting every month, and he obtained copies of the Constitutions used by other active Dominican communities in Europe from his provincial in France and was able to help Mother Catherine connect with other communities. Fr. Theissling, O.P.,[56] the Master General, encouraged them to continue along their path.

The general upheaval in Russia which kept the Communist government concerned with other matters, allowed the Byzantine Catholics to engage in dialog or "unification efforts." As was mentioned earlier, the Byzantine Catholics firmly believed and rightly so, that they were the means that God would use to reconcile the Russian Orthodox with Rome. The greatest fear the Orthodox had was that the Church would force them to become Latin rite. It was well known by them that certain bishops had indeed tried to force Latin rite practices on Eastern rite

---

[56] Fr. Theissling had spent several years in St. Petersburg, Russia, and was very interested in these Sisters.

Catholics.[57] "This is our constant tragedy. There is a secret decision on the part of the Poles that is as clear as day: the Eastern Rite is a temporary evil (the words of the Deacon Zelinsky) which must be destroyed. No unity of the Churches, just interrelations with individuals and their Polonization.[58] This tendency makes itself seen more and more clearly...." These ideas had existed for centuries and unfortunately one still finds them among Latin clergy, especially in Russia. Fr. Ignaty, who seemed to be so supportive of them, showed his true colors after the erection of the Russian exarchate. As Mother Catherine explained in a letter to a friend: "He has done a lot of harm since the time that the Russian Catholics formed an independent group."[59]

---

[57] There are many examples in both Europe and North America. One of the most notorious incidents was the efforts of Bishop John Ireland (St. Paul, MN, 1838-1891). He had a distinct dislike for the Greek Catholics in his diocese and beginning in 1891 tried to expel all the Greek Catholic priests in his diocese and impose Latin rite priests in their place. This caused literally thousands of Greek Catholics to turn to the Russian Orthodox Church.

[58] What Mother Catherine means here is that most of the Polish clergy wanted to enforce Polish Liturgical and religious customs on the Russian Catholics.

[59] Parfentiev, 85-86.

Another incident that hindered the dialog was the fact that certain priests had persuaded Pope Pius XI to issue the decree "Ea Semper" in which he said that everyone was free to choose whether they remained Byzantine Rite or became Latin rite. Many letters flew to friends in Rome. Mother Catherine wrote a long letter[60] to Princess Maria asking her help to convey certain documents from Exarch Leonid and Fr. Vladimir to the Pope which explained to him the real situation. The following excerpts give us a clear idea of what was at stake.

> The foundation stone of all our cause was the idea of a single whole Russia, keeping its heritage intact, and with its Eastern Liturgy, with its hierarchy united to the Roman See. It is on this basis, and only on this basis, that conversations can be conducted with the Orthodox clergy and with the best representatives of Russian society. In support of this notion another equally important idea has been advanced: that the Pope

---

[60] Mother had the Exarch read the entire letter for his approval before she sent it.

desires and loves Russia in its Eastern Rite, that he values her cultural and religious achievements: its deeds, its elders, all its eastern color and way of life; and that because of this he not only desires but demands that every Russian support his Rite, since it has enormous value; and that therefore a Russian cannot convert to Catholicism, he can only achieve fulfillment of what was deformed by correcting all mistakes....To support this they cited the encyclical "Orientalium Dignitatis," by which any Latin priest who tried to convert an easterner to acceptance of the Latin rite is subjected to the severest penalties, and so on. There are also the laws of the Propaganda Fide, which require that if there is a case of someone transferring from the Eastern to the Latin Rite that person is required to petition the Holy See. Therefore the Holy Father values a single, Orthodox Russia and desires this unity in a single Rite, not recognizing its being divided into eastern and western Catholics. This position was so firm that no one had ever protested against it or against its desirability.

The papal declaration "Chacun est libre de choisir son rite selon la conscience" upends all this position of ours and affirms the position of the enemies of Catholicism, alienating those who are friendly toward us. Liberty of choice of Rite means dividing the Russians into two camps in the religious sphere, camps which unfortunately have been enemies toward one another—examples are Galicia, America, and Russia. Not one Russian Orthodox patriot is about to agree to this. At the present moment the words of the Holy Father have especially painful associations for many people because they come at a time when the Eastern Church is torn between the old Church, represented by Tikhon and those around him, and the so-called "living" Church.[61] It is especially important in this regard, to demonstrate that genuine Orthodoxy

---

[61] Because the new Patriarch refused to go along with the Communists, they found those among the clergy who would support them and thus started a "new" Orthodox Church which they called the "Living Church."

is Catholicism, maintaining a single, united Russia, with its Rite, hierarchy, and so on.

At the beginning of my correspondence with you, thanks to the activity of Fr. Vladimir there were quite friendly feelings toward the Pope and toward Catholicism, as the embodiment of the idea about which I wrote above. Then began the time of suffering of the Orthodox Church: the seizure of its property, schism. At first Rome was viewed as a support, but the Bolsheviks, with the nose that they have for the satanic, immediately filled their newspapers with news about the agreement reached between Rome and the Bolsheviks about the entry of Jesuits and other Latin rite orders into the country 'to instruct young people,' and about the freedom these same orders had to propagandize Catholicism. All Russian society recoiled from Rome in disgust.

Samarin and his crowd basically insist that the shooting of Orthodox priests is done practically at the insistence of the Pope of Rome, who also supports the "Living"

Church! To all this one could say what a foreign acquaintance of ours said: "The way things are now, just as the return of the old regime in Russia is impossible, so it is just as impossible to unite the Churches. There is no one to unite with. The Pope is always 'up to date' and therefore his declaration about 'freedom of choice of Rite' fits with the times: there can be no question of unification of the Churches, but rather only of proselytism. Individual conversions come first." It needs to be taken into account that the positions of Fr. Leonid and Fr. Vladimir definitely restrained the Poles in their policy of Polonization and in their scorn toward us. They were able to affirm with conviction that the Pope *wanted* for Russia to be Eastern Rite, and that we Russians are the true representatives of Catholicism for the Russian people. The Polish priests were always suspicious about this support of Rome's for the Eastern Rite.

And it must be remembered that in Russia this is not just a question of Rite, but also an issue of politics and nationality. Poland and the Polish clergy do *not* want the unification of the Churches and most of all *they do not at all want* Catholic independence for the Russian Church of the Eastern Rite, answering only to the Holy See. The Eastern Rite must be destroyed and smothered—and smothered it will be, unless there is a miracle. Russian converts must be Latinizers and Polonizers. Such conversions are to be desired because they will increase Polish influence in Russia and lessen any chances for the hated Eastern Rite and for the conversion of Russia.[62]

    When Fr. Vladimir told his Vicar, Fr. Nikolay, that the Holy Father had refused everything contained in the two main points of our mission's needs, Fr. Nikolay exclaimed: "What can this mean?" Fr. Vladimir answered, "Expiation, Fr. Nikolay"... Yes, we can consider it expiation for our age-old sin of schism

---

[62] There is no evidence anywhere that Mother Catherine was anti-Polish. Her grievance here is not against Poles, but against the attitudes and actions of certain Polish clergy. It is to be remembered that some of her closest friends were Polish, as well as some of the Sisters. Indeed, as Mother related in one of her letters to Princess Maria, the Polish Sisters specifically offered their lives to God to make reparation for the hard feelings that existed on both sides.

and for all the sins of our unhappy, tormented Russia. But certainly not everyone is capable of taking on himself such penance. This is not a mission, not an easing of the way; rather it makes it more difficult to accept the Truth.

Moreover, it seems to me that all the information about Catholic affairs in Russia comes by way of foreigners, chiefly Poles. Such information is very dubious; and that if the Holy Father knew the real situation of the Catholic Church in Russia he would not act as he has![63]

Despite these setbacks, the Unification efforts taking place in Moscow were quite successful because in this city the Byzantine Catholics were considered "our own people" and not "agents of Polish influence."[64] As mentioned earlier, the Russian Orthodox had elected their own Patriarch, Tihkon, while the Communists were trying to erect their own "living Church" with those Russian Orthodox clergy

---

[63] Parfentiev, 87-94.
[64] Ibid., Appendix II, Unification Efforts, 177.

who were willing to go along with them. In order to honor the patriarch on his patronal feast day and show their allegiance, all representatives of almost all the parishes in Moscow held a special celebration. Fr. Abrikosov was chosen to represent the Byzantine Rite[65] along with several members of the parish. Everyone was astonished when upon entering the Hall, the Patriarch went first to Fr. Vladimir and greeted him warmly. Fr Vladimir gave him the present they had prepared for him—a framed copy of the prayer for unity by Pope Pius X. Fr. Vladimir told him how honored they were to attend and show their allegiance to the head of the Russian church. The Patriarch replied by saying he supported the dialog for unity with all his heart and gave it his blessing. He too prayed constantly for Church unity and blessed those who worked for this cause.

As a result of this celebration, regular meetings began to take place between the Byzantine Catholics and the Russian Orthodox. The Exarch was

---

[65] The Russian Byzantine Catholics regard the Russian Patriarch as head of their Church, just as other Eastern rite Churches have their own head, but all united under the See of Peter.

able to be present at these meetings as well. At first they took place on Russian Orthodox premises and at the first meeting a Latin priest was present, which caused the Russian Orthodox to express their displeasure. They asked that there be no Latin clergy present at their meetings. The second meeting took place right after the Pope's decree "Ea Semper" and there was considerable anger on the part of the Russian Orthodox at this turn of events. One of the Russian Bishops who had spent time in Canada spoke of the bad treatment Byzantine Catholics endured from the Latin clergy. Fr. Vladimir and the Exarch replied that unfortunately such things have happened, but were able to show by various statements of the Popes that they never approved of such measures.

After this it was agreed that the meetings should take place at the Abrikosovs. This was fortuitous, as it enabled the Russian Orthodox to see how they kept the Byzantine Rite in all its purity; that they used the same books, vestments etc. as the Russian Orthodox and there was not the slightest hint of Latinization whatsoever. This encouraged the dialog very much. In all there were five meetings and a sixth meeting was planned but other events occurred which prevented any more meetings from happening.

One of those who attended the celebration for the Patriarch was actually an agent for the GPU and he took note of all those who attended. Later the GPU came to the Abrikosov apartment while fortunately Fr. Vladimir was away and they spent several hours searching for incriminating evidence.

In April of 1922 a large group of Russian Orthodox clergy who had taken active part in the meetings were arrested. At dawn on August 17th the GPU arrived while the Sisters were chanting Lauds and arrested Fr. Vladimir. Other members of the parish were arrested as well in the following days. The GPU showed up at all hours to carry out searches and large waves of arrests of priests, professors, artists, authors, etc. followed each. The Sisters never knew when they would be next, but they knew their turn would come. Yet they experienced great joy because it seemed that God was accepting their vow of sacrifice for Russia.

Fr. Vladimir was sentenced to death by shooting, but this was commuted to exile abroad. He and 160 prominent writers, scholars, and intellectuals whose ideas the Bolshevik government found objectionable, were sent into exile on the so-called "philosophers' ship." They traveled by way of St. Petersburg where Fr. Vladimir was able to meet with the Exarch who gave him messages for Rome. Everyone thought the exile would be for a short time only, no more than 3 years at the most. No one thought Communism would last for so long. The Exarch gave him a much needed document which would allow him to offer the Divine Liturgy outside the Exarchate. Fr. Vladimir left on 29th of September and arrived in Rome in December. He informed the Papal Commission "Pro Russia" which was taking care of needs of Catholics in Russia on the state of affairs and suggested ways to help them. The Pope appointed him procurator for the Exarch and he was able to correspond with Mother Catherine for some time.

After the arrest of Fr. Vladimir, Fr. Nicholas took care of the Liturgy but other than that he was not much help to the Sisters and parishioners. Being timid by nature, he was barely able to stand the stress they were all undergoing. That meant that the burden of the Byzantine community now fell on Mother Catherine's shoulders and she herself had been suffering from bad health for some time. Being separated from her husband took its toll on her. It had been possible for Mother Catherine to leave with Fr. Vladimir and she went through a great struggle to turn down this opportunity, which we see reflected in one of her meditations on the "Seven Last Words."

> Into the life of every soul that has made the decision to attain complete purification no matter the cost, doing this to open the way for God's action in it—meaning the firm, unshakable decision to do all it is able on its part and to leave the rest to God—into the life of every such soul

comes a turning point, the time of the great renunciation. At first this means a renunciation of the self. Next, renunciation of the most cherished, dearest being, to which the soul may be attached in the very noblest way. This being may even be the one who led it to God. Taking pleasure and joy in the hold this being has over it, the soul was itself elevated to God, praising him and giving thanks. But it loved just this being and no other. It was good to be together, and some very indefinable, very fine thread, hardly noticeable, held it attached to this being and no other. The soul had spent a long time persuading itself that it was ready to give up this being for God's sake, ready to surrender it, but that this attachment really did not hinder its movement toward God. Rather it furthered it. Being with this created being evoked in it spiritual joy, the wish to speak of God, to serve Him. But suddenly, not entirely comprehensibly even for itself, a disquiet commences in the soul; an inner voice, the voice of grace, firmly and insistently tells it, at times depriving it of peace, that it is still not completely free, that this is still an attachment, albeit a very exalted one, and that it is only God who must rule, no one and nothing else. There is only God for those who wish by way of the cross and the wounds of Christ to go directly toward mystical death in order to then rise again to the blessed life of union. God is undivided unity, and He does not tolerate the least division or separation in the being which He has chosen for His own. This represents a high degree of attainment of purification: the soul completes the last stage of turning its whole being toward God, with no glance backward or to the side, with a complete detachment from what is very fine, very exalted, but none the less earthly, finite, and created. There is only God. How many souls come to this turning point in their spiritual life, to the final renunciation of the dearest, closest, and most beloved being, to whose spiritual rebirth and growth they have perhaps given so much strength that it has become their favorite child? They feel no, it's impossible, and say to God: "Just not this, Lord. Some other time, later..." But an irrepressible voice inside them stubbornly insists: "No, precisely this, and right now…There is only God." In the spiritual life one must fear self-deception most of all, and we must ask God to evoke in us a holy disquiet, insistently repeating to us what it is He desires. And then, finally, with the help of His grace we find sufficient strength in our self to carry out this final detachment from all created, finite things.[66]

The time after Fr. Vladimir's exile and threat of arrest was a time of doubts, vacillation and darkness for Mother Catherine. But no one ever saw this struggle; outwardly she was the same joyful, peaceful and kind Mother as she always was, the one to whom everyone went with their own struggles. At this time she chose for her motto: "Christ did not descend from the cross, but rather He was taken from it dead." In a letter to Fr. Vladimir she wrote:

> I am very weary, I am sick of everything, and the one thing I would

---

[66] Parfentiev, Appendix III, "Seven Last Words," 191-192.

give a great deal for is to be in your place…things are impossible in this country. There is simply nothing to breathe….I feel terribly alone and alien in our parish, even with the Sisters….In the first place there is simply the desire to see you, to talk with you, about everything that goes on, and not just about our cause or for the cause, just about everything. In the second place there is a thirst just to run, to run off without looking back. For my nature, everything and everyone here is simply unbearable. What a blessed time it was when I had the influenza, when I could be perfectly justified in seeing no one, as if I lived outside that company which always surrounds me.[67]

Suspecting that his time of arrest was also near, Exarch Feodorov gave instructions to various priests, telling them among other things to turn to Mother Catherine as she "merits full and absolute trust."[68] Patriarch Tikhon was arrested in April and

---

[67] Parfentiev, 115-116.
[68] Ibid., 122.

placed under house arrest for "anti-Soviet and counterrevolutionary activities." Since Archbishop Cieplak was fully supportive of the dialog between the Byzantine Catholics and the Russian Orthodox he was suspected of being a co-conspirator, together with his vicar, Fr. Konstantin Budkevich. On April 20, 1923 Exarch Feodorov, Archbishop Cieplak and Fr. Budkevich were arrested and condemned to death. They were taken to Moscow for the trial which enabled Mother Catherine to visit the Exarch in prison. International furor followed the arrests to such a degree that the Communists decided to make some compromise by exiling the Archbishop and shooting only Fr. Budkevich.[69] Exarch Feodorov was sentenced to the Solovki[70] prison.

The GPU continued their constant searches and now put listening devices in the apartment

---

[69] His cause was one of those introduced in 2002 and the Dominicans in St. Petersburg have a relic of him which is highly treasured.

[70] Once a monastery (and now restored), this was the most notorious of the prisons where the Communists sent the majority of priests, bishops, and religious. It is on one of the Solovetsky Islands in the White Sea.

rooms. On November 11, 1923 after 9 pm the GPU came again and kept up a search which lasted all night. Sister Philomena describes this episode: "All of the Sisters were gathered into one room. Some read, others prayed. All of them were entirely calm. Sr. Lucia (Anna Kirillovna Davidyuk) crawled under a desk and slept peacefully almost till morning. Mother Catherine and half of the Sisters were arrested. This same night Fr. Nikolay and many of the parishioners were also arrested."[71]

Several days later the rest of the Sisters except Sr. Catherine Ricci Elder and two other Sisters to take care of her (Sr. Catherine of Siena the Second and Sr. Hyacinth), were arrested and taken to Burtyrka Prison. Sister Catherine Ricci Elder was dying of brain cancer, yet she displayed an amazing degree of presence of mind before the police. Sister Josafata relates:

---

[71] *Journal of Sister Philomena*, first unedited translation by Professor Joseph Lake, TOP, (of the original hand-written copy was that used for the translation.) 13.

She was an outstanding nun. By nature she was clear thinking, direct and simple, and she pursued her goals uncompromisingly. As a young woman she was already fully mature in her spiritual life. She dedicated herself entirely to Christ, but calmly and methodically, without excesses. Shortly after our arrest the GPU issued an order that our parish house be seized. The three remaining Sisters occupied one room together. Sr. Catherine, even in this state of health, showed a calm spirit. Lying in bed she defended before the representatives of the regime their right to their own things and to the things which belonged to the Dominican Sisters, and a right to the library and to the apartment. Thanks to her energetic defense the authorities did not seize everything. Sr. Catherine ordered that the rest of the things be taken away, and as quickly as possible, to people they knew, aiming to sell them later and help the Sisters in exile with the money from the sale. Also thanks to her good sense and wise direction the younger Sister got permission from the authorities to take the things used for services to the Latin Rite church, the Church of the Immaculate Conception.[72]

The Sisters at first were all put in solitary confinement, as the GPU hoped this would break the Sisters. When this didn't work, most of them were put into cells with common criminals. Later Mother Catherine and some of the others were taken to Lubyanka. The filth, lice, and cold were small hardships to deal with compared to the interrogations. The rule of the prison required them to speak as quietly as possible and the guards had holes by which they could constantly keep watch inside the cells.

The only way for prisoners to communicate with one another was by tapping on the walls or the pipes, although this bore heavy penalties if one were caught at it. There was a special alphabet of these signs for communicating. The men were more uninhibited about resorting to this

---

[72] Parfentiev, 137-138.

method. The nuns resorted to it very rarely. With the help of this type of communication one could find out who was confined where or who was being interrogated, as well as about numerous other matters of importance to the prisoners. It was in this way—specifically by tapping on the pipes of the central heating system—that Sr. Catherine de Ricci Younger communicated with Donat Novitsky. Fr. Novitsky would tap out passages from the Sacred Scriptures for her. She was very grateful to him for this, since she was in solitary confinement, and had been threatened with being shot. It was by tapping in this way that it was decided that once a week, on Thursday after supper, each Catholic would, in addition to making his regular examination of conscience, make a general examination for the entire week with the intention of rendering thanks to God in this way. The Sisters told all the prisoners about these spiritual practices, and the parishioners communicated with one another, in this way maintaining contact over the course of their entire time in prison and in exile, even though they were all sent to different places. The majority of the Sisters who were confined at the Butyrka were, with the exception of Srs. Osanna, Joanna, Philomena, and Antonina, placed in one room together. This took place during Lent of 1924. Sitting in their cell they tried to lead the regular spiritual life of the order, praying the Dominican service together half aloud. They all said the rosary and the stations of the Cross together.[73]

As true Dominicans, the Sisters tried as much as possible to keep up their religious observances, praying the Liturgy and other prayers at certain times during the day. They were not permitted to do spiritual reading, so the older Sisters continued instructing the younger Sisters, especially those who were still novices preparing to take their vows. Many times the Sisters were offered their freedom if they would agree to give up the Byzantine Rite.

---

[73] Ibid., 128.

What stands out about Mother Catherine in prison is the deep love she showed to everyone. The common women criminals who were used to living in a bestial state seemed to be transformed just by being with Mother. As Sister Philomena writes:

> Mother Catherine was unaffected and unassuming with all these women, gentle, tender, understanding, and loving. They were lost souls, completely without morals and sullied by every imaginable crime. They were accustomed to mistreat anyone who had been arrested for something other than regular crimes, and especially those who had been arrested under the 58th—political—statute. But they loved M. Catherine. They became truly attached to her. The cell was gradually transformed. The shouting, the fights, and the cursing stopped.[74]

Another Sister relates how even the interrogators felt touched by Mother Catherine's holiness. "What an interesting and charming

---

[74] *Journal*, 14.

personality your Mother is," he told her. "It's just too bad that she is not a Communist."[75]

Finally the Lent of 1924 came and the Sisters spent it preparing for whatever their future would hold, since they knew the time for the sentencing was close at hand. Mother Catherine preached the last Spiritual Exercises for Holy Week for them on the theme "Christ the Sacrifice." "Mother expressed herself this way: 'No doubt each of us in having come to love the Lord and follow after him often asked in her soul that Christ give her the chance to take part in his suffering. This moment has come. Make real your desire to suffer for him.'"[76]

Then came Easter, a Feast of tremendous importance in Russia. "M. Catherine and the Sisters were now sure that the Lord had accepted their vow of self-sacrifice on behalf of Russia. They understood their arrest, captivity, and whatever was to follow as the answer to this vow, and as granted them by God's

---
[75] Parfentiev, 133.
[76] Ibid., 131.

mercy. He was giving them the good fortune to be able to join in the redemptive suffering of His cross. All of them were therefore full of joyful inspiration and courage, calmly awaiting whatever was to come."[77]

The feast of the Lord's Resurrection had arrived. It was celebrated movingly and solemnly. Since there was no tablecloth the Sisters covered the table with a sheet and set out upon it blessed food, from the packages that had been sent them. They dressed in their festive white dresses. At midnight they began to chant matins, one of the most solemn services in the Eastern Rite. During it "Christ is Risen" is constantly raised to the Lord, and the soul is borne aloft on wings of joy to its beloved, Risen Lord.

Early on Easter morning the Sisters who had been placed apart from the others—Srs. Osanna, Joanna, Philomena, and Antonina, as well as Sr. Lucia Chekhovsky, a Latin

---

[77] Ibid., 131.

Rite Sister of the Congregation of the Holy Family in St. Petersburg—were summoned from their cell for relocation.

The Sisters who had been summoned were put into a neighboring cell. While they were being led in they saw the long prison table, covered with a sheet and set for the Feast. There, seated at the head, was M. Catherine. With her were nearly all the Sisters, each one dressed for the Feast in a white blouse and black skirt.

It is difficult to convey the joy of this meeting: after several months of separation, on the very day of Easter, inside these prison walls, which now had somehow ceased to exist for them. When they had prayed and sat down at the table, the cell doors flew open once again, and in marched another whole group of prison officials, evidently making an inspection tour of the cells. The Sisters stood up at once, as was the rule in prison. The authorities inspected them all in silence, the table set for the Feast. Suddenly, totally unexpectedly, they said, *"С праздником!* (Best wishes for the Feast)." This was like a gift for them all, totally unexpected. In times such as those one could expect no kindness of any sort. For this to have happened made the mood even more joyous.[78]

A few weeks later, on May 19, 1924, the prison officials arrived in the cell with the papers with each Sister's sentence. There were never any court proceedings. Each Sister, instead of reading her own sentence, handed her paper to Mother Catherine, who then read the sentence out loud. After Mother had read the last sentence the Sisters sang the Te Deum. Then each Sister knelt in turn and renewed her vows in the hands of Mother Catherine. Three of the Sisters pronounced their vows for the first time, having made their novitiate in the prison. After this, "The Sisters renewed the special vow which they had made of sacrifice for Russia."[79]

---

[78] Ibid., 132.
[79] Ibid., 133.

Most Sisters were sentenced to 3 to 8 years of internal exile in Siberia, but at this point the place was not specified. They did not find out until they were on their way. Mother Catherine was sentenced to 10 years in prison as head of the "Moscow counterrevolutionary organization" in strict isolation. Sister Catherine de Ricci Younger to 10 years in prison, Sister Rosa of the Heart of Mary and Sister Agnes, 5 years in prison, Sister Imelda, 8 years in prison in Solovki and Sr. Dominica, 5 years in prison, also Solovki. The Sisters had to provide their own needs for the journey. They had next to nothing with them but God took care of them in a special way by means of the dying Sister Catherine Ricci Elder.

> Sr. Catherine Ricci Elder got all the things which the Sisters needed ready. For each of them she prepared a large sack which could be carried over the shoulders: three or four changes of underwear, two changes of clothing, a pillow, and also a little food. This was all of our Sisters' baggage—true monastic poverty. And how pleased they were later to have received these

sacks. They later thanked Sr. Catherine from their places of exile. The material circumstances of our Sisters were truly dire. Only the Papal Mission of Aid to the Starving provided any suitable aid for all those in need—It was thanks to this help that Sr. Catherine was able to give the Sisters the things required for their journey and to provide food for the children.[80]

As soon as they could the Sisters tried to contact each other from their own place of exile and to keep in touch with Mother Catherine who had been put in the notorious prison in Tobolsk, together with some of the other Sisters. Several Sisters also lived there as exiles and tried to visit them and bring them much needed food and clothing. However after a few months this was forbidden. Prison life wreaked its havoc on Mother Catherine's health which was already miserable (among other things she had tuberculosis, inability to digest prison food, migraine headaches and enlarged heart.) Her own family, the

---

[80] Ibid., 138.

Abrikosovs, were unable to help. The only recourse that was successful in the long run was for the Sisters to turn to the Political Red Cross.

The Political Red Cross, its official name being "Committee for Aid to Political Prisoners," had been organized by Ekaterina Pavlovna Peshkov, wife of the Soviet author Maxin Gorky. It existed from 1920-1937 and assisted Poles and other Catholics who had been imprisoned with food, medicines, clothing, and whatever help was needed. Ekaterina Pavlovna took a personal interest in Mother Catherine and all the Sisters, for which they always sent letters of thanks.

Mother Catherine remained in the Tobolsk prison until the middle of 1929, when she was transferred to the special political prison at Yaroslavl. Because the prison at Yaroslavl was of the strictest regime, it was dangerous for Mother Catherine to contact anyone; therefore she did not do so. Sister Catherine Ricci Younger was in this same prison, but during the six years they were there, they never once saw each other. Her influence upon the other prisoners being so great, she was considered an obstacle to all the Communists were trying to do in breaking down and degrading the prisoners. Mother Catherine kept herself and her cell in the neatest and cleanest condition she could. The prison authorities were dumbfounded that anyone could still strive to remain human in dehumanizing conditions.

There were quite a number of Catholic priests in this prison and it happened that during the daily allotted walks, Mother was able to speak with them in passing. The one whom she saw most frequently was Fr. Theophile Skalsky and even though the prison guards walked directly behind them, Mother was able to go to confession to Father by speaking softly. This was a great blessing because according to canon law of the time, no priest could hear confessions outside his own diocese without special permission. Father explained in a letter, "Having been in Kiev, on the boundary of the Mogilyov diocese, I had received such jurisdiction (to hear confessions anywhere) from the late Bishop Tseplyak, unlimited as to time and with the right to authorize other priests as well."[81]

After his release and transfer to Poland, Father wrote up his memories of Mother Catherine and sent them to Fr. Vladimir. Father writes:

> Anna Ivanovna, with her deeply religious spirit, endured her harsh lot as a Soviet convict with unimaginable calm and humility. She endured enormous privation, and terrible want in the area of food and clothing. However, no one heard from her a single word of murmuring or complaint. She asked me to find out your address and to let you know that she considers herself fortunate to have been able to endure so much for Christ and for the good of the Church. And if the Lord God deems it fitting to once more lay this cross upon her, she is always prepared to take it once again upon her shoulders. She has never had any regrets, and she

---

[81] Ibid., 147.

is always happy in the memory of all that has fallen her lot in Catholicism.

I personally consider her a true Confessor of the Faith, one who must be very dear to the Lord's Heart, and a being who brings joy among all the baseness of life in our day. She was not allowed to correspond with anyone, as I also was not. She received packages extremely rarely, and these were the very poorest. The Dominican Sisters who were scattered all over the place, would sometimes manage to be able to give her something. She would receive a little money sometimes from the Red Cross, but it was impossible at that time to buy anything with it in Yaroslavl, and she therefore lived in a state of total deprivation.[82]

Mother Catherine had confided to Fr. Theophile that she thought she had a tumor in her breast. He advised her to tell the prison authorities, which she did. She was then sent in May 1932 to Byturka Prison in Moscow for surgery as this prison had a hospital attached to it for prisoners. The

---

[82] Ibid., 146-148.

operation for breast cancer was considered successful though it left her left arm completely useless. Because of this as well as her bad health, Ekaterina Pavlovna was able to obtain an early release for Mother Catherine from the prison system. What joy and surprise Mother Catherine received when on the 30th of August she was informed that she was free and could live anywhere she wished "minus 12", meaning not in the 12 most important cities of the Soviet Union. She was given 10 days in which to find and prepare a place to live. Several Sisters already released from prisons were also living in Moscow, although Mother did not know it at that time. It being morning when she left the prison, she headed straight for the only Catholic Church open in Moscow, the French Church of St. Louis.[83] To her greater joy Mass was in progress and for the first time since 1923 she was able to receive Holy Communion.

The celebrant of the Mass was Bishop Pie-Eugène Neveu who having heard of Mother

---

[83] This Church belonged to the country of France, as part of the French Embassy, and therefore was outside Soviet jurisdiction.

Catherine, had been trying to get permission to visit Mother Catherine in prison. He was the Apostolic Administrator of Moscow for the Catholic Church and did tremendous deeds in trying to help all people. Since the Exarch was still in prison, Bishop Neveu was the head of both the Latin and Byzantine rite. Because of this, the GPU constantly surveilled him and tried to prevent him from carrying out his duties. He was a Frenchman and a member of the Assumptionist order. This religious order was founded with the special intent of laboring to promote the union of the East with the Catholic Church. All the priests of this order, which were few in number, were located in Russia and labored actively to help the Eastern Catholic clergy. Neveu was consecrated bishop in 1926 and appointed Apostolic Administrator in Moscow. In time he became the effective head of the Catholic Church of all Rites in Russia: "After the GPU learned of his consecration the authorities forbade him any pastoral activity, under threat of expulsion from the USSR. Only the firm position taken by the French ambassador saved him from this fate. It was the

French ambassador who used his influence to protect him."[84] The Bishop wrote later of Mother Catherine.

> Yesterday when I arrived at the church of St. Louis on Sunday I met, to my great astonishment, Mother Abrikosov. We introduced ourselves, of course. At the end of May she had been transferred from Yaroslavl to Moscow. Here, at the Burtyrka prison, she was operated for cancer, in June….This woman, a true Confessor of the Faith, possesses enormous strength of spirit. Next to souls like this one, one feels oneself to be a real dwarf. She still looks very bad; she is able to use only her right arm—the left one is disfunctional."[85]

Sister Philomena was also at Mass that day and she could scarcely believe her eyes when she saw Mother Catherine. Mother Catherine spent a few days with her and Sister Philomena took her to meet Ekaterina Pavlovna so she could thank her in person

---

[84] Parfentiev, 149.
[85] Ibid., 150.

for all her help while in prison both for herself and the Sisters. Mother was able to go to daily Mass as well, and one day after Mass while she was praying, Bishop Neveu came up to her with a young lady saying: "Mother, here is another daughter for you."[86]

This young lady from Kostroma was Minna Kugel, a convert from Judaism, whose family had threatened her in many ways if she became a Catholic. Earlier several of the Sisters had lived with the Kugel family for about three years, which is how she encountered Christianity for the first time. She was baptized into the Eastern rite by Fr. Sergei Soloviev, nephew of the philosopher Vladimir Soloviev. She took for her baptismal name Teresa in honor of St. Thérèse.

Mother Catherine decided to go to Kostroma where Sister Margaret and Sister Antonina were still living which enabled Teresa to come and see her every day with the hope of entering the Sisters.[87] At

---

[86] Ibid., 151.
[87] She eventually did enter and persevered until death.

first Sister Margaret was worried, knowing how the GPU was watching and that Teresa might be one of their agents. But Mother Catherine replied: "For the good and salvation of a single soul I am willing to go to prison for another 10 years." Then she repeated, "To save the soul of this child, Teresa, I am prepared to go to jail again for 10 years."[88]

But Sister Margaret's worries soon changed to worry about Mother Catherine. Clearly the cancer was still there and growing. Mother Catherine had to return to the hospital in Moscow every two weeks. Several of the Sisters managed to be in Moscow during one of these visits and there was a joyous reunion with Mother for Sisters Margaret, Imelda, Dominica, Hyacinth and Philomena for a few short hours. Sadly it was an obvious fact that Mother was not going to be with them for much longer. Mother took advantage of each trip to visit with Bishop Neveu and go to confession and Holy Communion. She also visited her family on one trip, who were very glad to see her again.

---

[88] Parfentiev, 152.

On one of her visits Ekaterina Pavlovna told her: "'I advise you to apply for an exit visa'.—'I have no intention whatever of leaving Russia.'—'Then you risk being arrested again'.—'Why?'—'Because you do not refrain from what I have spoken to you about.'"[89] What Ekaterina Pavlovna was referring to was that any mention of religion was cause for arrest and imprisonment. Her continued correspondence with Fr. Vladimir was especially incriminating. But Mother was not concerned; she was in God's hands. Let Him do whatever He wished. One of Mother's last letters was written on July 1, 1933, just before her last arrest "and it attests to not just her readiness for martyrdom and her love for the Sisters, but also to the fact that she placed a very high value on her link to the Dominican order and her membership in it."[90] It was written to one of the prioresses of a monastery outside Russia, presumably in Poland.

> Esteemed Mother, allow me to express my warmest appreciation in

---

[89] Ibid., 153.
[90] Ibid., 154.

the name of all my Sisters and in my own name for your remembering us, for your prayers, and for your charitable aid. Dispersed and forcibly separated, at times deprived of any spiritual support, subject to persecution and constant harassment on the part of the Bolshevik government, so brutal and cruel, my Sisters draw strength from the thought that you pray for them and that you love them in a spirit of Dominican unity, which is so essential for us as a support in all our sufferings. I myself unfortunately cannot rely on helping them in any way other than by my prayers, since living in exile, which has been extended by three years, I am separated from my beloved daughters. Additionally, correspondence is not always possible in this unhappy country, since a letter with spiritual content constitutes sufficient basis for being sent to prison. But fortunately I am ill, and my fairly serious illness causes them to grant permission to go to Moscow from time to time for special treatment. Thus I have the good fortune not just to receive Holy

Communion and go to confession but also to see, encourage, and support some of my younger Sisters. Do not think, Mother, that we complain of our fate or that we are unfortunate. To the contrary, we thank God that He has granted us this high honor, the opportunity to suffer for Him. Our only fear is that we are unworthy of this calling. And so I beg you, Mother, to pray that we be made worthy of being thus chosen. At the present moment all my Sisters are divided into three groups: those who are at liberty, those who have been sent off to exile, and those who have been imprisoned. But I am glad to tell you that they nonetheless live an intense life, full of dedication, a life that is entirely Dominican. Once more, Mother, please accept my gratitude and, of course, pray for us. We greatly need your prayers. May I also be excused for requesting that you send me three copies of the Rule[91] (the new edition). I would be greatly obliged. Please

---

[91] The GPU had seized all their books, etc., including their Rule and Constitutions during their many searches.

accept the expression of my profound respect for you. Sr. Mary Catherine[92]

---

[92] Parfentiev, 154.

WITH JESUS ON THE CROSS

Finally an event occurred which led to Mother's new arrest. In Moscow there was a very devout Catholic lady named Camilla Nicholayevna Krushil'nitskey, a close friend of Bishop Neveu. She often held discussions in her apartment for young women "who were not satisfied by Marxist ideas and who were interested in the question of the existence of God." Bishop Neveu approved of these meetings, but the GPU kept a close watch, waiting for the right moment. One of the young women was Anna Brilliantov, who couldn't make up her mind what to accept. On one of Mother's visits the Bishop introduced her to Camilla Nicholayevna and the latter invited Mother to come to the meetings. Mother accepted and then asked Sister Philomena to come with her. Sister was horrified at the idea, knowing how the GPU had spies everywhere, but felt she should go with Mother. There were 3 meetings altogether that Mother was present at between June 20th and July 1st, 1933. On July 27th the GPU arrested Camilla Nicholayevna and Anna Brilliantov and several others. On the 5th of August Mother Catherine was arrested in Kostroma and brought back to Burtyrka Prison. In a few days Srs. Dominica, Joanna, Teresa (Kugal), Margaret, Magdalen, Philomena, Veronica and Vera, the former Sister Maria Rosa[93] were brought to Moscow as well.

The GPU had improved their methods of interrogation and torture, especially in psychological pressure. Some Sisters signed anything just to get away from prison and into a camp. One Sister died from the torture. The main accusation against them was that they were creating a terrorist group determined to assassinate Stalin. Poor Anna, despite not having any faith, was treated as criminal as well.

---

[93] Sister Maria Rosa, one of the first Sisters, while caring for a dying woman during their first period of exile, became attached to the husband while trying to console him in his grief. She bitterly regretted this and after his early death petitioned to be readmitted to the Sisters. They sent her petition to the proper authorities who refused it. Nonetheless she remained close to them until her death.

They all received their sentences on February 19, 1934. Camilla Nicholayevna and Anna were both sentenced to Solovetski where in 1937 they were both shot. Mother Catherine was sent back to Yaroslavl and the others to labor camps or exile in Siberia. Attempts were made to have Mother exchanged and then exiled outside of Russia, but Bishop Neveu knew Mother would never accept. "As far as Mother Abrikosov is concerned, I am quite certain that she would not leave here without a formal order from Rome: she would rather die in prison than permit that her daughters learn that she was safe while they remained in such a terrible situation. Nonetheless the serious condition of her health would justify that such an order be given. At least if she were abroad she would be able to receive the Sacraments and live the life of the Church. Here she is deprived of all that. However I have every reason to suppose that she will remain in prison "usque ad mortem"—right up to her death."[94]

---

[94] Parfentiev, 162.

No word was heard from Mother Catherine from prison. The Sisters and Political Red Cross tried in vain. The Sisters in Yaroslavl would take packages as often as allowed, but whether Mother received them was anyone's guess. Finally on June 23rd the Sisters were told that Mother had refused their packages, and on August 2nd they were told that Mother had died. No one knew for years on what day Mother actually died. Not until the KGB released the prison records in 2002 did the actual date become known, which is June 23th, 1936. Her body was cremated on the 27th of July,1936.

> Evening has come. At the cross "a great stillness" reigned. It is the day of the Sabbath, on which the Lord rested from His works…Jesus looks peacefully and clearly to heaven and says softly, as He had as a child: "Father, into Your hands I commend my spirit." And saying this He bowed His head and gave up His Spirit."
> And He will come at the dawn of the third day, shining in glory, to bring the soul, joyful and free, into His bridal chamber. But for the time being He

has left it to rest: it has suffered together with its crucified God, it has struggled, and in spite of everything, in spite of all the lying temptations of the devil, the world, and the flesh, it has remained believing, it has hoped, it has loved. And now is its victory. It has conquered the world. Now, together with its Lord, it has merited its rest.[95]

---

[95] Parfentiev, Appendix III, "Seven Last Words," 206.

Conclusion

The Sisters continued to live their religious life as best they could. They spent most of the following years going in and out of prisons, labor camps and exile. Yet they received these sentences with joy, seeing in them the fact that God was accepting their vow of sacrifice. As Sister Philomena relates: "Only the constant help of the merciful God, combined with prayer offered with deep faith and devotion, could preserve in their souls profound peace and the willingness to bear all that God would send to test them—to bear these trials which He sent as proof that he had accepted the vow the Sisters made of self-sacrifice on behalf of Russia."[96] Mother Catherine had enjoined on them the practice of having the oldest Sister living in the house be the superior. This became a great grace and blessing for

---

[96] *Journal*, 16.

the younger Sisters. Whenever and wherever it was possible the Sisters tried to live together as a community, while continuing to work for a living.

The priests who were pastors of the French church of St. Louis in Moscow also acted as spiritual directors of the Community and helped them maintain ties and communication with the Vatican and the Dominican Curia. From time to time Fr. Michel Florent, O.P., from Leningrad, would also come to visit them. After Mother Catherine's death Sister Stephania was appointed as Prioress of the Community. In 1946 Maria Filippovna Sokolovsky entered the Sisters at the age of 45. She had been wanting to join them for a long time but circumstances prevented it. In 1947 Fr. Antonio Laberge, pastor of St. Louis, appointed Sister Antonina as prioress.

In 1955, two years after the death of Stalin, the Soviet government rehabilitated all political prisoners and all those Sisters who survived were able to return home to Moscow. There were only nine

Sisters left by this time. Sister Teresa (Mina Kugel) had found work in Lithuania after the War, and since it was much easier in this country for her to attend Church, she was able to get government papers that allowed Sister Philomena and Sister Lucia to come as well. One day in Church they met Sister Imelda, prioress of the Dominican contemplative nuns (there were only five as all the Polish Sisters had left). She made arrangements for them to move into a small apartment across the street from themselves. Soon all the other Sisters moved to Vilnius as well, except Sister Stephania and Sister Catherine who remained in Moscow.

The Sisters remained faithful to all Mother Catherine had taught them, and kept up close contact with the Byzantine Dominican Laity in Russia. Eventually two men, influenced by their example, joined the Dominican Order, and were ordained as Dominican Byzantine priests.[97] Both these priests are

---

[97] Fr. George Friedmont is a Third Order priest and Fr. Evegeny Heinricks, OP, was the first pastor of St. Catherine's parish from 1990, when it was returned to the Dominicans, until 2002. Both are still attached to St. Catherine's.

still living, as well as Dominican Laity who knew the Sisters. The last Sister died in 1993, but their memory lives on and is cherished by all Byzantine rite Catholics in Russia.

During the years of Communist persecution the Dominican Order did everything it could to help the Sisters. Since the cause of Mother Catherine and Sister Rosa of the Heart of Mary was introduced in Rome, it has been our hope that the Order will once again take interest in them. This is necessary if their cause is to advance. With the publication of the life and work of Mother Catherine in English in the near future, it is hoped that Dominicans will come to know about these brave Dominican Byzantine women and be inspired by them to such a degree that they will spread the word! And what better time than this Year of Faith, for the Order to know of Mother Catherine Abrikosova, "a true confessor of the Faith." ✷

PHOTOGRAPHS FROM MOTHER CATHERINE'S LIFE

Anna (left) with cousin Vera (right)

Anna Ivanovna Abrikosova
(Mother Catherine)

The Abrikosov Family at The Oaks,
their summer residence.

Ivan Ivanovich, Vera Nicholaevna, Anna Ivanovna, Aleksei Ivanovich, Sergei Nicholaevich, Boris Ivanovich, Aunt Vera, Uncle Nicholas Aleksandrovich Pavel Nicholaevich, Augusta Nicholaevich and Nicholai Nicholaevich. Dmitirii Ivanovich and Khrisanf Nicholaevich are standing.

Five of the sisters at Moscow in the
early days.

Sr. Monica, Sr. Antonina and Sr. Catherine Ricci the younger

Prayer for Beatification

of Mother Catherine Abrikosova

Anna Ivanovna Abrikosova

O God Almighty, Your Son suffered on the Cross and died for the salvation of people. Imitating Him, Your Servant, Mother Catherine Abrikosova loved You from the bottom of her heart, served You faithfully during the persecutions and devoted her life to the Church. Make her famous in the assembly of Your Blessed, so that the example of her faithfulness and love would shine before the whole world. I pray to You through her intercession, hear my request.... Through Christ Our Lord. Amen.

About the Author

Sister Mary of the Sacred Heart, O.P., is a contemplative, cloistered Dominican nun living in the Monastery of St. Jude in Marbury, Alabama. Growing up on a farm in upstate New York, she always dreamed of being a published author, but this is her first published book. Her interest in Russia has inspired her research into the lives of Dominicans who lived and worked in Russia.

In 1991, the first article about Dominicans in Russia was published in English, which led Sister to begin research into their lives. In 2002 Sister spent three months in Russia learning the language and culture, while exploring the possibility of a Dominican monastic community in Russia someday. During her stay she was able to meet some of the people who knew the Byzantine Dominican Sisters personally.

Dominican Nuns
of the Monastery of St. Jude
Marbury, Alabama

St. Dominic founded the Dominican Nuns in 1206 so that their contemplative life would be at the heart of the Holy Preaching of his Order. Founded as the first interracial cloistered monastery in 1944, the Dominican Monastery of St. Jude is situated in the heart of the Deep South (Alabama). Praying "That All May Be One" the nuns as Guards of Honor of Our Lady each have a daily Hour of Eucharistic Adoration and Rosary. They strive to live the Total Consecration to Jesus through Mary, and sing the Divine Office each day, using the traditional Dominican Latin chants for the major Hours and Compline.

For more information please contact:
Dominican Nuns
Dominican Monastery of St. Jude
143 County Road 20 East
Marbury, Alabama 36051
email: stjudemonastery@aol.com
website: www.stjudemonastery.org

Made in the USA
Charleston, SC
04 October 2013